Andrew has got home. He is in a
bad mood.

"Had a good day?" his mum says.

"Don't ask!"

"What's gone wrong?" she says.

"Everything!" he says.

"First, I missed my bus.

The driver saw me running.

He just drove off.

That was a great start to the day!"

3

"I had to wait ages for the next bus.
Then it started to rain and I got soaked.
I nearly froze to death!"

"Surprise, surprise, I was late for school. Everyone in the classroom stared at me. It was so embarrassing!"

7

"I couldn't do my maths.

It was really hard.

Rachel started laughing at me.

That did my head in."

9

"At dinner time, I was sent to the back of the queue.
The dinner-lady said I was pushing.
She had a right go at me.
It wasn't fair!"

11

"Then it was PE.
I didn't have my trainers and
Mr Jones shouted at me.
And ..."

13

"… I'm getting a great big spot!"

"Hey, cheer up!" says his mum.

"You're making me depressed!

Shall I tell you some good news?"

"NO! I DON'T WANT TO KNOW, OK?"
shouts Andrew,
and he stomps up to his bedroom.